Quiet City

Quiet City

P O E M S

Susan Aizenberg

 B k M k P r e s s
University of Missouri-Kansas City

BkMk Press
University of Missouri-Kansas City
5101 Rockhill Road
Kansas City, Missouri 64110
(816) 235-2558 (voice)
(816) 235-2611 (fax)
www.umkc.edu/bkmk

Missouri
Arts Council
The State of the Arts

Financial assistance for this book has been provided by the
Missouri Arts Council, a state agency.

Cover Painting: "Untitled No. 124" by Michael David
Author photo: Jeffrey Aizenberg
Book design: Susan L. Schurman
Managing Editor: Ben Furnish
Associate Editor: Michelle Boisseau
Executive Editor: Robert Stewart

BkMk Press wishes to thank Cynthia Beard, Elizabeth Gromling,
Marie Mayhugh, Brittany Green, Kristin Pugh.

Library of Congress Cataloging-in-Publication Data
Aizenberg, Susan.
 [Poems. Selections]
 Quiet City / Susan Aizenberg. -- First edition.
    pages ; cm
 ISBN 978-1-886157-98-9 (acid-free paper)
 I. Title.
 PS3601.I94A6 2015
 811'.6--dc23

                                    2015010986

This book is set in Garamond and Baker Signet.

A refuge, permanent, with trees that shade
When all the other cities die and fade.

—Weldon Kees,
"To Build a Quiet City in His Mind"

for Jeffrey

Acknowledgments

Heartfelt thanks to the editors of the following publications in which these poems first appeared or were reprinted, sometimes in slightly different versions or with different titles.

AGNI New Poets Series: Take Three/2 (Graywolf Press): "Cleaning the Bank" (in chapbook section *Peru*)

Alaska Quarterly Review: "Chatham Bay"

Blackbird: "Things That Cannot Be Compared," "July at Rose Blumkin," "The Unloved Beautiful," "Eleanor Writes She's Reading Rimbaud"

Burnt District : "Mornings," "Toward an Autobiography of My Imagination"

Chance of a Ghost (edited by Gloria Vando and Philip Miller, Helicon Nine Editions): "Capote in Brooklyn"

Connotation Press: An Online Artifact: "Dust," *A Poetry Congeries* edited by John Hoppenthaler: "Wind"

The Drunken Boat: "Red Goose"

Hotel Amerika: "Capote in Brooklyn"

Hunger Mountain: "My Mother as Orpheus"

Iowa Woman: "Cleaning the Bank"

The Journal: "Evening," "For a Long Time I Have Wanted to Write a Poem About Happiness"

"Eleanor Writes That She's Learned *Good Jailing*,"
"What You Couldn't Say"

Midwest Quarterly Review: "Lake Mascoma"

Nebraska Presence: An Anthology of Poetry (edited by Greg
Kosmicki and Mary K. Stillwell, Backwaters Press):
"Things That Cannot Be Compared"

Poetry Forest, China, and *Chinese-Western Poetry*, Macao: "Things
That Cannot Be Compared," "To Vishniac," and
"Capote in Brooklyn," translated into Mandarin by
LuYe

Prairie Schooner: "I-80," "Eleanor Underground,"
"To the Mother of the Sixteen-Year-Old Boy
Shot Dead by the Police After She'd Called Them,"
"Lake Mascoma," "To Vishniac"

Provincetown Arts: "LuYe: Rapeseed Fields" (Portfolio
edited by Philip Brady)

Spillway: "Via Negativa," "Everything That Rises"

The Untidy Season: *An Anthology of Nebraska Women Poets* (edited
by Heidi Hermanson, Liz Kay, Jen Lambert, and
Sarah McKinstry-Brown): "Late Nineteenth-Century
Romance"

I am grateful to Creighton University and the Nebraska Arts Council for fellowships that helped me to research and write many of the poems in this book, and to my colleagues at Creighton, especially those in the creative writing program—Dave Mullins, Brent Spencer, and Mary Helen Stefaniak—for their friendship and support.

For encouragement, support, multiple readings of these poems and much more, I am happily indebted to Erin Belieu, Carol-Lynn Marrazzo, Anna Monardo, Betsy Sholl, Pamela Stewart and Jean Valentine. Most special thanks to Maura Stanton. My gratitude to my family is unending.

Finally, heartfelt thanks to Michelle Boisseau, Ben Furnish, Susan Schurman, and everyone at BkMk.

Quiet City

III

I

Wind

This evening rough winds blow the surface of the river.
 The starlings and purple martins have flown
to quieter skies. Clouds scud like fast ships
 across a horizon blue as the heaven my Jesuit friend

Bill believes awaits the forgiven, and from downriver,
 gusts carry the sounds of Playing with Fire, a tribute
band whose soupy Hendrix covers echo off the concrete
 façade of the loading docks and merge with the rising

shrieks of children playing in the park. Bill and I drink wine
 on the balcony, and in this mild August light,
the Missouri gleams as it rolls, ancient and dumb, south
 beneath Kerrey Bridge swaying on its slender cables.

Two nights ago, there was a killing on the Iowa side,
 the fifth in the city this summer. Some argument
among strangers, a gun. To the west, the squat Omaha
 skyline glimmers. I imagine this river before

its toxic dumps and gangland bodies, its shoreline
 we've reclaimed as this tidy riverscape, where now no sign
of the murdered man remains, when all that answered
 the water's slow passing was the swish of wildflowers

in the long prairie grasses, the rustle of foxes
  and the rabbits they hunted. Bill believes the souls
of the dead are like the wind, that we can see them
  everywhere in what they touch and carry. He tells me

we can hear them now, in the plangent closing notes
  of "Hey Joe" and the cheers of the crowd borne
up on the air's invisible currents, as they travel
  out over the riverbank, beyond the sun-struck highway.

Via Negativa

I'm sure they meant no harm,
the good Quakers—

believing as they did in sorrow
and redemption—

when they imagined
into being Eastern State,

the world's first true penitentiary,
where for decades prisoners

never saw the sky, lived in silence
so complete, it must have been

palpable as the stone floors
of their cells. My father, too,

believed in the power
of *true regret* and sentenced

my mother sometimes to weeks
of silence. How cheery he was,

with my brother and me,
in those long hours after dinner,

the meat and potatoes
square meals of the early '60s

I could never swallow.
Later, when she thought

we were sleeping, I'd hear her
through the thin bedroom walls,

Please just say something, I'm sorry—
you were right, I was wrong.

I knew even then what I'd heard
in her voice was fear. His steps

when he left for work in the morning
were soft as the muffled tread

of the Eastern State guards
in their felt slippers, the wheels

of their carts wrapped
in cotton wool. Locked in

for years, the petty thieves
and drunks mostly went mad,

though some learned, as my mother
did, to speak whatever words

might release them into the world
of sound and the small,

necessary, consolations of even
the coldest human speech.

My Mother as Orpheus

Shameful, the worn suitcase
  and borrowed fare, the smuggled
    cheese and bread, four days'

hidden meals for her; for me,
  she paid—scrambled eggs
    three times a day, the coach car's

cheapest rations. Kind waiters
  smiled at her, knowing
    there'd be no tip, and shameful,

too, their kindness. Back home
  they'd said she was crazy to chase
    him in her *advanced condition*—

brazen belly and no man,
  a chatty toddler—no keeping
    secret the reason for our travel.

The train carried us past endless
  fields and farmsteads, miles of crops
    my Brooklyn mother couldn't name,

all the way to Reno, glittering
  wilderness of never-closed casinos
    and pawnshops, the Holy Grail

of the big score spiraling down—
  the used cars for sale on every corner,
    fresh stakes for tapped-out gamblers.

Late Nineteenth-Century Romance

after William Merritt Chase

When he revised its title from *The Tiff*
  to *Sunlight and Shadow*, the painter hoped
we'd first admire his use of shape and color,
  this lyrical *en plein air* scene redolent
of midday heat and fragrant grass studded
  with wildflowers, that we'd imagine the thrum

of enervated yellow jackets, the *shush, shush*
  of wind-stirred leaves. But it's this woman
and this man that arrest me, and surely
  as if this were a page from Wharton or
a Browning monologue, I can read in their stopped
  bodies the familiar narrative of their despair.

He may be a banker or a businessman,
  come home for tea to find his new bride languid
as a doll in the costly hammock. He's grown weary
  of her melancholy, though her ankles crossed
in soft leather boots, his gift from their Italian tour,
  continue to arouse. Clearly they are rich,

the woman in servant's black in the background
  no more to them than the barrel she tends.
It would be easy to despise them. And yet
  something eloquently human inheres

in their frozen gestures—the man's ruddy profile
  and the litter of cigarettes at his feet evidence

of his impatience, something cruel in the proprietary
  drape of his arm across the chair back.
And though she does not turn to face him,
  we can see the woman listens, her one visible eye
dull with sorrow. Where her mouth should be,
  just the porcelain shell of her curved fist.

Mornings

Before the train screamed him through tunnels
to his windowless office, the idiots
he had to "sir," my father needed a space
without us, so in a crack of light from the bathroom,
he dressed, held his shoes by two fingers,
and left us sleeping. That walk

to the diner, the last stars fading out,
the sky lightening from black to blue to white,
was his time. He walked in all weather,
let each season touch him all over,
lifted his face to rain and sun. He liked
to watch the old houses stir awake
and nod to the woman in her slippers on 27th,
smoking as she strolled her little mutt.
To step back, smooth as Fred Astaire,
from the paperboy's wild toss.

Milk bottles sweated on doorsteps,
sweet cream on top, and once, he lifted a quart
from its wire basket, drank it down
beneath our neighbor's winking porch light,
and left the empty on the stoop.

Eleanor Underground

Nebraska, 1996

Autumn and the leaves look edible.
  You drive the awninged morning streets,
    your mouth puckering at the sweet and sour leaves—

sugary blood oranges and tart lemons,
  here and there, a cardinal red startling as a shout
    among the drowsing shotgun houses.

We'll say it's a town not far from Rulo,
  where the crazy trailer-park prophet made
    of a six-year-old's tongue an ashtray,

of his tattooed Judas a tanned hide. He paces on death row
  now—biblical grey beard, pale eyes pinballing.
    A town off the highway Starkweather cruised

in the fifties, *season of the witch*, death
  as a teenager dressed like James Dean in jeans
    and leather, duck's ass and Cuban heels.

A town that thinks of itself as solid,
  a place like TV's Mayberry, where Aunt Bee
    and the girls live, sexless in cotton housedresses,

all that female mess of milk and blood and the touch
   of men behind them, made-up just a little
      for each other now. A town where the neighbors

imagine no one needs to lock their doors,
   where small town Christianity cradles them
      in its white Midwestern hands. Not the kind of place

where a girl, who dresses like a boy the girls laboring
   in factories and packing plants want to cling to,
      respite from the smack in the face and beery quickies

they know as *dating*, is raped and shot.
   Remind yourself you can't afford to feel superior.
      You're a woman with secrets, this trip

one more lie you'll have to tell.
   Watch your speed and drive with care.
      You're just another citizen passing through.

Cleaning the Bank

A.J. dances the industrial-sized vacuum
around the locked and shining desks,

while our baby presses
half-circles of oil from his palms

onto the beveled glass door.
I swipe, over and over, at the streaks

on the other side with a gritty chamois,
the high-pitched smell of ammonia

raking my throat. The invisible night-crew,
we scrub the johns and empty ashtrays,

stale smoke and flurries of dust
and ash shrouding our clothes and hair.

And it doesn't matter that it's dirty work,
or that years from now this moment

will crumble to shabby nostalgia,
that we'll divorce, and our child will drift,

until he's distant as these tellers
and customers we never see. For now,

we're almost happy. We're singing along
as the Velvet Underground pulses

from our almost-paid-for jambox.
Our voices echo off the vault's cool steel.

I-80

He looks ill, the young man huffing
along the shoulder, his chin tucked hard

into the collar of his worn jacket.
His breath smokes and blows

above his bare head in this January wind
that gusts the powder off buried fields

to glaze the shivering barbed wire.
At seventeen, my son walked

twenty miles along this highway,
darkness shrouding these ranches,

sting of ice on raw skin through holes
in his sneakers. All afternoon I'd refused

to come get him from the bar where his girl
had ditched him, rough voices

and country jukebox in the background,
each call more panicked.

That was the year of bail bonds
and rehab, the orange jumpsuits

of County Correction, weeks I shopped
for pounds of macaroni and cheese

until he said it made him sick—
and wasn't that what I'd intended?—

and paid the rent on a basement apartment
where, after pawning first the radio

and then the TV, he cried for hours
each day. *No*, I said, call after call,

shivering in the dry heat of our living room,
as I watched ice blind the windows

and pictured him walking these same miles
of road, where now I lose the man

just past the mile marker. It glares behind me
as I accelerate through coils of snow

whirling across the frozen blacktop.

To the Mother of the Sixteen-Year-Old Boy Shot Dead by the Police After She'd Called Them

How could you have guessed he was so afraid   of
returning to jail   he'd pull the gun you didn't know he
had   or that the cops   young men themselves   would
shoot him neatly in his thin chest   not wound his leg
or use gas   or a stun gun—didn't they do that first?
What could you have done but call them   when he
broke probation   all that screaming   fists in the walls,
your younger boy   weeping as he waited for the school
bus   your husband packing his bags? Who sacrifice
as your house turned combustible around you   and
he slept all day, crawled   through a window in the
night to smoke dope   and drink, pass out   on the
front lawn at 3 A.M.   too heavy by then for you to
drag him in to bed   his face in the morning so like
the one   you knew and loved   so like the one   you
watched   in that second before they shot him   the
moment stilled   to stop-time   his mask of anger
softened   into something   you can't name   something
that leaves you now   unable to speak or move—

Lake Mascoma

New Hampshire, 2001

Like shades ascending, this morning's fog
rises above the wind-ripped silk

of the shallows, then fades
like the rasp of summer BMWs

as vacationers hurry past our end of the lake
for Dartmouth's tonier beaches.

Not far from here, the bones of Shakers
resolved to dust lie blessed in simple

boxes. Humble before an exacting God,
like Jews they interred their dead

without flowers. What remains of my father
also lies in unvarnished pine, the glint

of medals my grieving brother laid
on its lid more wreath than they'd permit.

Morbid, I wonder what's left of him
beneath Miami's ravening sun, the burnt

grass my mother weeds from his plot
in Beth Israel cemetery. Before the funeral,

she lifted her skirt to show me the lace
wedding garter beneath her mourning blacks.

Ann Lee believed herself bound for Heaven.
My father believed only in Hell.

Now a jade cathedral shadows
the far shore near the Shaker graveyard,

and I see the glow of torches—no,
it's just the mountain as it pierces the mist

and our neighbor's running lights. He hoists
the glimmering flag of his catch, *hello*,

a man heading home, neither symbol nor sign.

II

Toward an Autobiography
of My Imagination

She was born the day the babysitter
  locked me in her storeroom for toppling
    her boy's tower of alphabet blocks

and then coolly sucking my thumb
  as I watched him cry. She came to me
    in a dusty shaft of sunlight tunneling

through the one high window and promised
  my mother would find me, slap
    that sitter with her fierce left hand

and make her sleep for a thousand years.
  She grew in the damp salt nights of Miami,
    where my father was the click of dice

tossed on a bureau, and the dark a slow river
  where we drifted, unable to sleep,
    on the unsteady raft of a neighbor lady's

bed. She sang in the windy palm leaves
  and the cicadas' razor-whine.
    In Brooklyn, she guarded bathroom

doors as I was sick, then walked me
  past the alleys where black cats leapt
    from fire escapes and tightened

the stitches of my breath. She was there
  on those blue evenings I strolled
    beside my prodigal father along Avenue W,

where he'd name the galaxies and spin
  his war stories, tales of how with nothing
    but a compass rose and dead reckoning,

he'd shot the stars over the Atlantic
  and found his way home, and where I learned
    to love the way that lies could shape

the constellations burning out
  above the city into a navigable shimmer,
    a celestial map she'd teach me how to read.

The Unloved Beautiful

wife is perfect as a wedding cake,
a Hitchcock blonde

who knows something's up,
but this time she's not snooping,

just "tidying up" as women did then,
and when she finds in her faithless

husband's pocket a brass key,
she knows at once where it fits.

They're rich enough for a paneled study,
a man's mahogany desk—everything

is gendered, this is the early '60s—
and there she finds his divorce

papers, old photographs, a birth
certificate that says her name is a lie.

And I thought of you, Mother,
in that Flatbush walk-up,

just tidying up, when under
his rolled socks and Ban-Lon shirts

you found Father's cache
of Air Corps discharge papers—

his rank Second Lieutenant, not Major,
navigator, not bombardier.

Betty Draper screams and tears
at her husband's too-handsome face,

then leaves him for a life-raft
lover, but you, Mother, closed

that cheap drawer tightly, Pandora
sealing the lid to a wind-filled jar.

July at Rose Blumkin

memory unit, Home for the Aged

Even this early in the morning,
heat breathes heavily against the panes
and the light's a white flame that warps
the glass of this picture window
overlooking the "wander garden"

and its border of young maples and beyond them—
I swear—gravestones rising

from the mist in the cemetery
just across the road. We've arrived
to find your father dozing here,
in the television room, deaf
to the chattering loop of *Lucy* reruns

flickering the big screen and the rhythmic
nonstop barking of the woman

slumped in the wheelchair
closest to it. At ninety-two, his skin's
almost translucent and his arms
are mottled with bruises the bitter
purple of ruined eggplants, and nearly

that large, a sorry map of needle sticks
and places where he's rested too long

against his walker. When he wakes
he knows us, but not our names,
what year it is, or how to call up sense
and syntax from the ruptured channels
harrowing his brain. Not all

he says is gibberish: *This is the shits,*
he tells us. *We're not doing this again.*

A man named Buddy, still dapper
in pressed jeans and a turtleneck, agrees.
Some daughter must do his laundry.
Mostly the men and women here
are incontinent, and like your father,

mostly they refuse to eat.
The young nurses are kind,

some of them lovely, as they crush pills
into applesauce for spoon-feeding,
offer juice boxes, and speak softly
to their charges, who doze
and nod, tremulous as dandelion puffs,

on the stalks of their necks.
It's hard to leave, and you give your father

your hand, tell him how many days
it will be until you return.
He repeats the number, *three*,
and seems to understand, and though all
his life he was a man uneasy

with affection, now bends
to kiss your fingers, courtly and sad.

Evening

Winter evening, yellow lamplight, her mother stares at
       the dirty plates.
Winter evening, yellow lamplight, her mother stares at
       the dirty plates.
Her father bends to the child's homework, says, *Any*
       moron can see the answer.
Her father bends to the child's homework, says, *Any*
       moron can see the answer.
Winter evening, yellow lamplight. Her mother bends
       to stare at the dirty plates.
See the answer, says the child's homework. *Any moron*
       can, says her father.

We'll sit here all night until you get this. She hears her little
       brother's door shut.
We'll sit here all night until you get this. She hears her little
       brother's door shut.
Her mother does not speak, scrubs the knives and
       glasses.
Her mother does not speak, scrubs the knives and
       glasses.
She does not speak, hears her little brother's door
       shut. Her mother scrubs
the knives and glasses. *We'll sit here all night until you get this.*

Stupid, says her father. *You could get this if you'd stop crying.*
Stupid, says her father. *You could get this if you'd stop crying.*
"Any moron," her mother says, *means, "I love you most of all."*
"Any moron," her mother says, *means, "I love you most of all."*
Any moron could get this, Stupid, if you'd most of all stop crying.
Her father means *I love you*, her mother says.

All evening, yellow lamplight. Her mother scrubs at
       dirty plates.
The child bends to her homework. She hears her father.
"We'll sit here, Stupid, until you can see the answer" means *all*
      winter.
Her mother stares at the knives and glasses, does not
      speak.
Stop crying, says her little brother's shut door. *If you could*
      get this.
Any moron. I would love you most of all, says the night.

Chatham Bay

Here, stray tides gutter the dunes.
Since winter, the harbor's been at risk.
Pitch pine and scrub oak anchor
sandy grass, shape veiled dens
for the dun-colored foxes your camera

can't catch. Mornings, I hunt for china
cockles and cat's paws. You kneel
among Virginia rose and wild grape,
glittering fiddler crabs grown exotic
through your magnifying lens.

In my favorite photo from this summer,
I squint offshore to watch high tide,
the lonesome drift of Ashley Bar
going under. I'm the small figure shading
my eyes in the shadow of our rented

cottage. You're the dark shape I'm smiling
for beneath a bleached August sky.

LuYe: Rapeseed Fields

The Island in the Center of the Yangtze River

Everywhere on the island the rapeseed flowers
are in blossom. We should christen them *Official Flower*

of the Island in the Center of the Yangtze River.
It's April, and now they begin to understand the world.

Over and over they say *love* and *love*.
Even their eyelashes are golden. They speak in bright voices.

They make the sky dizzy. They cover the fields
like an enormous, outstretched coat painted

with yellow flowers by a country girl, its patterns
the wavering shapes marchers form, blooms plaited

in their hair and bouquets in their hands,
in a Flower Day parade. Here, the world's a floodlit stage,

singers trilling classic opera. Soon it will darken
as the show ends. The audience applauds,

the curtain lowers. Then the little flowers will bear
the oil-rich seeds, deep in the vaults of their bodies,

and wait to be taken away, like new brides
to their husbands. When we walk to the end

of the yellow fields at the banks of the Yangtze,
the strong wind makes me suddenly lonely.

So many rapeseed flowers—
can they understand my northern accent?

—translated from the Mandarin with Jinmei Yuan

LuYe: Two Butterflies

A yellow butterfly and a white butterfly.

Prince and princess, they fly
from their blue morning flower

apartments. They fly over the field
and the pond where lotus blossoms

float. They fly over reeds growing
on the banks of the Yangtze.

They fly over the dirt road
and along the bean fields

and come to the banks of the Yangtze.
Southern butterflies, elegant

scholars thinking elegant thoughts.
Bourgeoisie of the island.

They wear thin silk shirts.
Softly, in their genteel language

they vow undying love. They sing
local opera. They recite

a poem entitled "The Butterfly
Loves the Flower."

One is Hon Fanguy, *Romeo*,
the other LiXiangun, *Juliet*.

The butterflies of my northern
hometown, Shan Dong,

are humble. They don't sing opera.
They don't write poems.

Followers of Confucius,
they recite the *Analects*.

These two flutter around us,
whispering. I ask a local man,

can you translate
this southern dialect

into Mandarin? Though I try
and try it seems I understand

only one sentence—
Look—the white butterfly says

to the yellow one—*that northern
woman looks so old-fashioned.*

—translated from the Mandarin with Jinmei Yuan

Red Goose

. . . the lowliest of my assigned duties was the one I liked most, dusting off the sample shoes in three brightly colored sample rooms each morning. . . .
—Tennessee Williams

Still just Tom at thirty,
he's one more unskilled worker

clocking in and out six days
each week, his life's brief measure

of hours lost to work numbing
as the old-time sermons

his mother drags him to—payback
for *ungallant* Sunday hangovers.

The world's largest shoe factory
is a vast, cacophonous machine—

rough thunder of metal presses
insistent as migraine, shrill of whistles

that signal time to come, to go,
time to eat, to stop eating—

until he wants to retch, to lie
for hours in a shuttered room,

chilled compresses smoothing
the lines from his forehead.

But that's his sister's luxury,
and so he hides out each morning

among the dazzling showroom
mirrors and the high-polished shoes

on their stacked glass terraces,
dusting and dreaming. Was he plotting

already his escape? His *desertion*
of Rose? I like to think he was,

that he imagined, perhaps,
a landlocked romantic's Cuba,

brown-skinned boys in straw hats,
soft lilt of Spanish on the air—

alma; mi corazón—machetes flashing hot
equatorial sun. Beyond the fields,

a warm, gator-green ocean. White sailboats
like doves tracing the horizon.

Capote in Brooklyn

Spring 1963

Back home from three years' *monastery life*, working
in Europe, he's in love with these pacific Heights
and genteel streets named for fruit trees that could
never grow here, with Willow Street, especially,

the yellow house where he lives with Jack,
where each dawn they hear—amazing!—a cock crow
from some neighboring yard. Mornings he walks
the Esplanade above the docks and the traffic

seething below towards the city, the *tall dazzle*
of its skyline a jagged brilliance rising from the East River.
He notes the flower man with his archaic dull horse
and cart, the young mothers pushing carriages,

their candy-cotton hair teased high, and makes his way
to the end of the docks, where the neighborhood
shifts into abandoned warehouses and dim alleys,
where there's a haunted hotel, a fabled ghost who passes

each morning by a fifth-floor window. He's waiting,
unable to finish the book he knows will make him,
until the courts decide: *will they swing or no?*
They write him from their death-row cells.

He sends them cigarettes and books—dictionaries
for Perry, porn for Dick. *Swing or no*? Perry told him
Dick once ran down a dog on the highway for fun.
That's what kind of man *he* was. Not like him,

Perry said, he was never mean if he could help it,
made Mr. Clutter comfortable before he cut his throat.
The wind off the river smells of coffee and bait
from the trawlers, and the June mornings gleam.

Far west, a Methodist crypt amidst the wheat fields
and prairie flowers, the sealed Clutter house
also waits — for the living to claim what its dead
no longer have a use for: pie tins stacked and shining

on a kitchen shelf, a girl's locked diary buried
among schoolbooks, her father's boots ready
by the mud scrape. Beside a narrow bed, left where
he can find them in the morning, a boy's thick glasses.

III

To Vishniac

If only they'd been purely souls, saints,
or like the ditch weed thriving
against the ghetto wall, could have survived
on air and sunlight alone. You knew

from the first graffiti shrieking in the alleys,
the posters erupting on courtyard paling
and tidy storefronts—*Support Equality and Peace,*
Vote for Hitler—all over your beloved Berlin,

the corner bakery's window display
changed from dark loaves and sweet cakes
to what looked like antique radio
antennas—devices for measuring skulls,

sorting Gypsies from Mongrels and Jews,
Mongrels and Jews from Aryans—
your neighbors queuing up to certify pure
lineage—that already they were ghosts.

• • •

Faces framed in basement windows,
shoeless children and old men peer out at streets

they cannot enter. A cobbler idles beside
his empty bench. A young man,

homeless, carries all he owns in a paper sack.
Your ancestors, and mine, Roman,

a book of photographs I now hold in my lap.
Smuggled Leica hidden in your coat,

you shot these *ordinary stories*
of the vanished Jews of Warsaw, 1936.

Here, the shades of peddlers pace, out of habit,
or frail hope, behind bare stalls. Here,

a lucky porter dozes on the splintered
crate he's mule to, boots held tight against

his chest. A bearded rabbi listens
as his student, a boy so thin he might be ten

or seventeen, makes his case for an *ess tog*,
an *eating day*, meaning one more meal a week,

to make three. Your ancestors and mine,
Roman, though strange even to us

in their fur hats and medieval cloaks,
their queer tongues—the Yiddish

they made of fractured Russian, German,
and Polish their only country; the ancient

Hebrew prayers they chanted, *davening*—
the tranced rocking and keening, mumbled

or shouted songs offered up to a nameless God
who'd never shown them favor or mercy—

marking them *foreign* wherever they fled.
I wanted, you write, *at least to save their faces.*

* * *

No photograph records the rabbi's answer.
The caption tells us that the boy,

though *promising*—even there,
they spoke of *promise*—

could not study, that he thought only of food.
You did not photograph the rabbi's

Yes, the boy fallen, having fainted
in relief. One arm raised, palm up,

he's forever caught in eloquence, articulate
gesture, his sharp, familiar profile

my son's or yours, lively as a bird's.

Dust

When she woke in the morning, the only clean part of her pillow
was the outline of her head.
　　　　　　—Timothy Egan, *The Worst Hard Time*

I think it must have come to seem to them biblical,
　those seasons of *drouth*, the earth itself a glistering
anvil beneath bleached and empty skies, the sun's light,
　sharp as a blade, piercing the dried and naked stands

of honey locusts their men had set as windbreaks,
　withering their roses and pansies and the neat kitchen
gardens, bordered by mulberry hedges, they'd tended.
　No living green anywhere for the eye to rest,

they wrote their families back east, *nothing thrives*
　but thistle and insects, the damned rabbits. For miles
around them, nothing but abandoned farms,
　no crops to anchor the fields, and when *blow season*

came, the *big rollers* and *black dusters* bearing
　their rough freight of blown topsoil to blind
the cattle and scrape the paint off the barns, the air
　so charged with static a kiss or a handshake

knocked you flat, it must have seemed a plague.
　Sky black as the inside of a dog, the men said.
Blow your nose, your hand comes away black-snotted.
　Father Coughlin on the radio blamed the Jews

and bankers, but it must have felt like God himself
  was furious, and who could fathom God? Imagine
how they had to wake to it, morning after morning,
  a meal of dust sifting through the ceiling,

coating the turned-over pots and soaking through
  the wet towels veiling every surface. How it snaked
past the doorjams and window frames they'd sealed
  with newspapers and gummed tape, rags soaked

in kerosene. Imagine the blackened sheets
  and the gritty oil that filmed the water they drew
to wash them in, the layers of dust that rippled across
  their scrubbed floors, deep enough for dunes

they had to wake the eldest boy or girl each morning
  to shovel out, their mouths and noses masked
like small Jesse Jameses. And when the cattle began to die,
  and then the children, the frail sacs of their lungs

shredded and their stomachs swollen with dirt,
  some of them went sorrowing, *dust mad*,
through the vacant streets, but mostly, they endured.
  It's them I think of now, the ones who endured,

how they must have rested, so briefly,
  in the evenings, writing their letters home before prayer
and bed by the dim light of oil lamps, how they
  must have stared at the unstoppable dust rising

again in the darkening air, the way they
  must have breathed it in slowly, slowly out.

Things That Cannot Be Compared

—after Sei Shonagon

My father's hand, elegant as typescript, before his stroke. My mother's lefty scrawl, the way she underlined *We* on my birthday card—*We wish you much happiness!*—four months after his death. The deep green of this morning's lowering cloudbank, sea lettuce riding the Intertidal. Bleached sheet of the sky back home, Nebraska heat rippling above the stunned soy fields. Miraculous snowy egret, tall as a woman, feeding with genteel *sang-froid* on palm fronds outside my mother's kitchen window, so close we might have touched her swanny neck. Black bear cub last night, lost in the widening dark glade beyond the yellow hoops of porch lights, who would not be lured to safety by the game warden's stale doughnuts. Shrill song of gulls scavenging. The flutter and purr of Carolina locusts.

When one has stopped loving someone, one feels that person has become someone else, even though he is the same person.

Substitute *ghost.* *A question of mourning.* *Unable to mourn.*

Red hour of the wolf. No sound except the whir of fan blades above our borrowed bed, the silvery notes of my mother's wooden cuckoo. She believes it herald of my father's spirit. Each hour I hear its bright cry rising from its mechanical throat like the freed breath of

sleepers. It wakes me from my dream of her overlit kitchen,
the negative space before the window where my father is
not standing, transfixed by the egret, calling me to *Come, see!*
Where he does not wince as I join him, recoil from his kiss.

Eleanor Writes That She's Learned *Good Jailing*

As in: never accept contraband,

no photographs or cookies

across the Visiting Room table.

Leave them at the package room, she's learned

to remind her daughter. As in: wear

your ID badge all the time. No forks

or scissors in your cell. Don't sleep

through morning count. Don't daydream

and fail to hear your name called.

Find your inner *safe place* and go there

every time you have to squat,

cough, and let a guard look up

between your cheeks. Try not to let that

spoil each visit it follows. A pack

of cigarettes to the woman working

laundry will get you your sheets

back. Bad manners here not to close

your door when you undress.

Eleanor Writes She's Reading Rimbaud

No one's serious at seventeen.
—A. R.

I must confess, even though I know better than to get nostalgic,
   that his *beautiful nights* and *scents of vineyards and beer*—
      his *green lindens*—all of it—take me back, a little,

to those early years in Cortland, each fall the smell of apples
   like a sweet red fog all over town. We'd work a day shift
      at Smith Corona, lie in the dark fields at night. I can still hear

the cars rushing by on the highway, see the stars overhead
   fade with faint quiverings, so many more than I'd ever seen back
      in Brooklyn. It all seemed so romantic, the gun beneath the car

seat, a shoebox stash of acid and speed, a boy whose touch
   on a pool cue brought him to my room early mornings,
      flush with cash he'd taken off the dumb-bunny freshmen

at the college up the hill. I swear we even played that scene,
   tossing bills over ourselves, high and naked, in my narrow bed.
      I don't want to remember our lies, our petty thieving,

how we stitched kangaroo pockets into the linings of our coats.
   Or how for weeks we lived on boosted steaks and candy.
      I don't want to think again of next-door L., how her toddler

stared all day out the window above the crummy bar
  where she danced, while she and her junkie boyfriend slept off
    their latest *derangement.* All I ever gave that kid was a wave

of my hand. Still, some days that girl I was wants out,
  wants back her reckless nights and slow, stoned afternoons.
    —Sometimes the air is so sweet that you close your eyes—

What You Couldn't Say

for Eleanor

A story you burned to tell—
telephones all day, all night, voices
familiar or strange—the still

moments. Kitchen windows framed
a past you'd cultivated—roses,
a garden, disordered and homely—

just what you needed most, those first
days. No one was there to listen,
your last story bleeding through lit

branches, the yellow-tinged flames
of flowers. Your face was hot, your hands
cold, you had as much time

as you wanted: words you mouthed,
still bitter, your story untold, your luck,
like the grackles, heading south.

For a Long Time I Have Wanted
to Write a Poem About Happiness

A little at a time and slow is best . . .
—Weldon Kees

Across the street, ghostly hoists and tractors slowly dry
beside the skeleton of a new high-rise.

Storms have rinsed the summer air of the day's brute humidity,
and now, redolent of wet grass, it lifts the red perfume

of my geraniums from their clay pots.
The city's quiet, the hush of traffic along Pacific Street,

awash in motor oil and vapor light below us,
almost the only sound. Leaves drip from the sugar maples,

as one by one, our neighbors' windows illuminate
the facing apartments, gold squares in a blue-black quilt.

Everything That Rises

At the summit you will find yourselves united with all those who,
from every direction, have made this same ascent.
—Pierre Teilhard de Chardin

Suspended and swaying from steel cables, the bridge
seems to listen for some word from the river.

A ribbon of hammered nickel, you write, *see how it shines.*

You've made love with your husband and now
even the indigo skyline, still vague

out your window, seems to shift in its sleep.
It's nothing like the childhood landscape

you recall: the cool, dark sand of Brooklyn
beneath splintering boardwalks, first kisses, feral cats

gliding like shades through the steam rising
from the subway to catch the wind, the wind

broadcasting the bright sounds of the Temptations
and Four Tops from transistors all over town.

You don't want to know just blocks from here
three tweakers are cutting up a comrade they believe

holds out on them, don't want to imagine the silvery
gleam of tape gagging his mouth, his slow death

ten minutes' drive from where your son's
child rises, wet and smiling, from his crib.

Because she knows your habits, your mother calls
from her pink condo beside the ocean.

She swears your dead father was there
when she woke, that her enormous cockatoos,

don't you dare laugh, are intelligent, that when they heard
her stir, they began to sing. You picture her faded

nightgown, the sultry air troubling the curtains,
how she stands, phone in hand, watching

the wide gulf, a lowering astonishment of yellow moon.

Notes

"Via Negativa" is inspired by Robert Hass' magnificent poem, "The World as Will and Representation."

"Mornings" is for Edward Singer.

In imagining Eleanor's world in "Eleanor Underground" and the other Eleanor poems in this volume, I found the following books especially helpful: *Diana: The Making of a Terrorist*, by Thomas Powers; *Family Circle: The Boudins and the Aristocracy of the Left*, by Susan Braudy; *Kent State: What Happened and Why*, by James Michener; *Life on the Outside: The Prison Odyssey of Elaine Bartlett*, by Jennifer Gonnerman; *Marking Time: Letters from Jean Harris to Shana Alexander*, by Jean Harris; *SDS*, by Kirkpatrick Sale; *The Sixties: Years of Hope, Days of Rage*, by Todd Gitlin; and *With the Weathermen*, by Susan Stern.

Ann Lee in "Lake Mascoma" refers to "Mother Ann Lee," prophet of the Shaker movement.

The television show referenced in "The Unloved Beautiful" is *Mad Men*.

"July at Rose Blumkin" is in memory of Morris Aizenberg.

"Evening" is for MDS.

"Red Goose" owes a debt to Lyle Leverich's *Tom: The Unknown Tennessee Williams*.

"Capote in Brooklyn" owes a debt to Gerald Clarke's *Capote: A Biography*.

Images in "To Vishniac" are occasioned by the photographs in Roman Vishniac's *A Vanished World*.

"Dust" owes a debt, for details of the experiences of Dust Bowl survivors, to Timothy Egan's *The Worst Hard Time* and to Caroline Henderson's *Letters From the Dust Bowl*.

Italicized lines in "Eleanor Writes She's Reading Rimbaud" are taken from Rimbaud's poem, "Novel."

"For a Long Time I Have Wanted to Write a Poem About Happiness" is for Jeffrey Aizenberg.

"Everything that Rises" is dedicated, with love and gratitude, to my mother, Edith Latman Singer.

Susan Aizenberg is the winner of the Virginia Commonwealth University's Levis Prize and the Nebraska Book Award for Poetry for her first book, *Muse* (Crab Orchard Poetry Series, Southern Illinois University Press) and is professor of creative writing and English at Creighton University in Omaha, Nebraska. She co-edited *The Extraordinary Tide: New Poetry by American Women* (Columbia University Press) with Erin Belieu and is the author of *Peru*, a chapbook that appears in *Take Three: 2/AGNI New Poets Series* (Graywolf Press).